I0087365

Glorious

You!

*Do you even **<u>realize</u>**
what you are?
Alphabet Soup*

A.   Amazing

B.   Breathtaking

C.   Cherished

D.   Divine

E.   Exquisite

F.   Fantastic

G.   Genuine

H.   High-Quality

I.   Important

J.	Just
K.	Kind
L.	Loved
M.	Magnificent
N.	Nice
O.	Outstanding
P.	Prized
Q.	Quality
R.	Rare
S.	Superb
T.	Terrific
U.	Unique
V.	Valid

w. Worthwhile

x. X-tra

y. You

z. Zesty

YES YOU ARE and
FOREVER WILL BE!!!

You are fantastic awesomeness, pure into infinity magnificence mixed with an amazing dash of superb marvelousness tossed by a very real, truly pleasant positive preciousness of essence that is treasured by my heart and is topped by your absolute divineness. I'm *always* full because my salad (*that is you*) is complete.

Shine,
Shine,
Shine!

SPLENDID

****

Is
what you
are.

Aaahhh

hhhhhh

h…..

Oooooo

OOOOOO

OOOO....

Magnificent
YOU

What's glorious about you?

You are my reason.

You are my favorite way to soar.

You are my favorite book.
You are my favorite feeling.
You are my favorite flavor.

You are my favorite song.

You are my favorite treasure.

You are my favorite adventure.

You are my favorite vacation.

You are my favorite hour.

You are very simply my _favorite favorite!_

You are a
KING
or maybe
You are a
QUEEN
or maybe
YOU. JUST.
ARE.

Greatness

looks
sooooo…
awesome on
you!

Truth and Wisdom Go

hand and hand with you

You are my favorite
gem.
You are my favorite
reason why.
You are my favorite
advantage.
You are my favorite
book.
You are my favorite
feeling.
You are my favorite
love song.
You are my favorite
flavor.

You are my favorite treasure.

You are my favorite way to fly.

You are my favorite adventure.

You are my favorite verse.

You are my favorite chapter.

You are my favorite song.

You are my favorite song.

You are my favorite
song.
You are my favorite
song.
You are my favorite
song.
You are my favorite
song.
You are my favorite
song.
You are my favorite
song.
You are my favorite
song.

You are my favorite
song.
You are my favorite
song.
You are my favorite
song.
You are my favorite
song.
You are my favorite
song.
You are my favorite.
Did I mention…

YOU
KEEP
HOPE
ALIVE!

Roses are red,
Violets are blue.

You are
glorious

GLORIOUS
YOU!

E-v-e-r-y single day you are glorious. Yes!

Day 1: You are incredible.

Day 2: You are a part of everything I do.

Day 3: You are my point.

Day 4: You are everything.

Day 5: You are a beautiful dream.

Day 6: You are my celebration.

Day 7: You are always.

Day 8: You are my wings.

Day 9: You are so beautiful to me.

Day 10: You have a kind heart.

Day 11: You are my bridge, my A to Z.

Day 12: You are my beloved.

Day 13: You are with me.

Day 14: You are thoughtful.

Day 15: You are believed.

Day 16: You are my hero.

Day 17: You are wonderful.

Day 18: You are my advantage.

Day 19: You are important.

Day 20: You are sincere.

Day 21: You are amazing.

Day 22: You are precious.

Day 23: You are cherished.

Day 24: Your love is delightful.

Day 25: You are the complete package.

Day 26: You are brilliant.

Day 27: You are as it should be.

Day 28: You are the one.

Day 29: You are entirely divine.

Day 30: You are breathtaking.

Day 31: You are GR88888888888888888888T TTTTTTTTTTTTTTT!!

I
I Love
I Love You
I Love You So
I Love You Soo
I Love You Sooooo
(take a breath)
I Love You Soooooooo
I Love You Soooooooooo
I Love You Sooooooooooo
(take a breath)
I Love You Sooooooooooooo
I Love You Soooooooooooooo
(take a breath)
I Love You Soooooooooooooooo
I Love You Soooooooooooooooooo
I Love You Soooooooooooooooooooo
(take a breath)
I Love You SoooooooooooooooooooooM
I Love You SoooooooooooooooooooooU
I Love You ooooooooooooooooooooooC
I Love You SooooooooooooooooMUCH!!!

(arms down)

You are my

Every Single Day

In

Every Single Way

♪♪♪ ♪♪♪ ♪♪♪

You are the song
that I sing.
With you I don't
worry about a thing.
You've got my back,
I've got yours too.
This is my song
from me to you.

♪♪♪♪♪ ♪ ♪♪♪♪♪ ♪
♪♪♪♪♪ ♪

♪♪♪ ♪♪♪ ♪♪♪

Knew all along you
were my song.
Knew from the start,
you're good for my
heart.
When I am happiest,
I'm with you.
When I'm with you
I'm singing a song.

♪♪♪♪♪ ♪

You are so Wondrous and I know it because...

you are brilliant
u r **W**onderful
you are so good
u r **S**unny
you are genuine
u r **I**ncredible
you are exquisite
u r **A**uthentic
you are divine

u r **M**arvelous

you are valuable

u r **A**ppreciated

you are sincere

u r **P**aramount

you are extraordinary

u r **G**ood

you are treasured

u r the **F**inest

you are just

u r **F**abulous

you are breathtaking

u r **W**orthy

you are the best

u r **B**rilliant

you

are

loved.

Do you know some thing?

You are
the
perfect
you!

AAAAAAAAAAAAAAAAAAAAAAAAAAAAAA
AAAAAAAAAAAAAAAAAAAAAAAAAAAAAA
AAAAAAAAAAAAAAAAAAAAAAAAAAAAAAY
AAAAAAAAAAAAAAAAAAAAAAAAAAAAAA
AAAAAAAAAAAAAAAAAAAAAAAAAAAAAA
AAAAAAAAAAAAAAAAAAAAAAAAAAAAAA
AAAAAAAAAAAAAAAAAAAAAAAAAAAAAA
AAAAAAAAAAAAAAAAAAAAAAAAAAAAAA
AAAAAAAAAAAAAAAAAAAAAAAAAAAAAA
AOAAAAAAAAAAAAAAAAAAAAAAAAAAAA
AAAAAAAAAAAAAAAAAAAAAAAAAAAAAA
AAAAAAAAAAAAAAAAAAAAAAAAAAAAAA
AAAAAAAAAAAAAAAAAAAAAAAAAAAAAA
AAAAAAAAAAAAAAAAAAAAAAAAAAAAAA
AAAAAAAAAAAAAAAAAAAAAAAAAAAAAA
AAAAAAAAAAAAAAAAAUAAAAAAAAA
AAAAAAAAAAAAAAAAAAAAAAAAAAAAAA
AAAAAAAAAAAAAAAAAAAAAAAAAAAAAA
AAAAAAAAAAAAAAAAAAAAAAAAAAAAAA
AAAAAAAAAAAAAAAAAAAAAAAAAAAAAA
AAAAAAAAAAAAAAAAAAAAAAAAAAAAAA
AAAAAAAAAAAAAAAAAAAAAAAAAAAAAA
AAAAAAAAAAAAAAAAAAAAAAAAAAAAAA
AAAAAAAAAAAAAAAAAAAAAAAAAAAAAA
AAAAAAAAAAAARAAAAAAAAAAAAAAA
AAAAAAAAAAAAAAAAAAAAAAAAAAAAAA
AAAAAAAAAAAAAAAAAAAAAAAAAAAAAA
AAAAAAAAAAAAAAAAAAAAAAAAAAAAAA
AAAAAAAAAAAAAAAAAAAAAAAAAAAAAA
AAAAAAAAAAAAAAAAAAAAAAAAAAAAAA

AAAAAAAAAAAAAAAAAAAAAAAAAAAA
AAEAAAAAAAAAAAAAAAAAAAAAAAAA
AAAAAAAAAAAAAAAAAAAAAAAAAAAA
AAAAAAAAAAAAAAAAAAAAAAAAAAAA
AAAAAATAAAAAAAAAAAAAAAAAAAAA
AAAAAAAAAAAAAAAAAAAAAAAAAAAA
AAAAAAAAAAAAAAAAAAAAAAAAAAAA
AAAAAAAAAAAAAAAAAAAAAAAAAAAA
AAAAAAAAAAAAAAAAAAAAAAAAAAAA
AAAAAAAAAAAAAAAAAAAAAHAAAA
AAAAAAAAAAAAAAAAAAAAAAAAAAAA
AAAAAAAAAAAAAAAAAAAAAAAAAAAA
AAAAAAAAAAAAAAAAAAAAAAAAAAAA
AAAAAAAAAAAAAAAAAAAAAAAAAAAA
AAAAAAAAAAAAAAAAAAAAEAAPAAAA
AAAAAAAAAAAAAAAAAAAAAAAAAAAA
AAAAAAAAAAAAAAAAAAAAAAAAAAAA
AAAAAAAAAAAAAAAAAAAAAAAAAAAA
AAAAAAAAAAAAAAAAAAAAAAAAAAAA
AAAAAAAAAAAAAAAAAAAAAAAAAAAA
AAAAAAAAAAAAAAAAAAAAAAAAAAAA
OAAAAAAAAAAAAAAAAAAAAAAAAAAA
AAAAAAAAAAAAAAAAAAAAAAAAAAAA
AAAAAAAAAAAAAAAAAAAAAAAAAAAA
AAAAAAAAAAAAAAAAAAAAAAAIAAAAA
AAAAAAAAAAAAAAAAAAAAAAAAAZZZ
ZZZZZZZZZZZZZZZZZZZZZZZZZZZZ
ZZZZZZZZZZZZZZZZZZZZZZZZZZZZ
ZZZZZZZZZZZZZZZZZZZZZZZZZZZZ
ZZZZNZZZZZZZZZZZZZZZZZZZZZZZ
ZZZZZZZZZZZZZZZZZZZZZZZZZZZZ

ZZZZZZZZZZZZZZZZZZZZZZZZZZZZZZZZZZZZ
ZZZZZZZZZZZZZZZZZZZZZZZZZZZZZZZZZZZZ
ZZZZZZZZZZZZZZZZZZZZZZZZZZZZZZZZZZZZ
ZZZZZZZZZZZZZZZZZZZZZZZZZZZZZZZZZZZZ
ZZZZZZZZZZZZZZZZZZZZZZZZZZZZZZZZZZZZ
ZZZZZZZZZZZZZZZZZZZTZZZZZZZZZZZZZZ
ZZZZZZZZZZZZZZZZZZZZZZZZZZZZZZZZZZZZ
ZZZZZZZZZZZZZZZZZZZZZZZZZZZZZZZZZZZZ
ZZZZZZZZZZZZZZZZZZZZZZZZFZZZZZZZ
ZZZZZZZZZZZZZZZZZZZZZZZZZZZZZZZZZZZZ
ZZZZZZZZZZZZZZZZZZZZZZZZZZZZZZZZZZZZ
ZZZZZZZZZZZZZZZZZZZZZZZZZZZZZZZZZZZZ
ZZZZZZZZZZZZZZZZZZZZZZZZZZZZZZZZZZZZ
ZZZZZZZZZZZZZZZZZZZZZZZZZZZZZZZZZZZZ
ZZZZZRZZZZZZZZZZZZZZZZZZZZZZZZZZZZ
ZZZZZZZZZZZZZZZZZZZZZZZZZZZZZZZZZZZZ
ZZZZZZZZZZZZZZZZZZZZZZZZZZZZZZZZZZZZ
ZZZZZZZZZZZZZZZZZZZZZZZZZZZZZZZZZZZZ
ZZZZZZZZZZZZZZZZZZZZZZZZZZZZZZZZZZZZ
ZZZZZZZZZZZZZZZZZZZZOZZZZZZZZZZ
ZZZZZZZZZZZZZZZZZZZZZZZZZZZZZZZZZZZZ
ZZZZZZZZZZZZZZZZZZZZZZZZZZZZZZZZZZZZ
ZZZZZZZZZZZZZZZZZZZZZZZZZZZZZZZZZZZZ
ZZZZZZZZZZZZZZZZZZZMZZZZZZZZZZ
ZZZZZZZZZZZZZZZZZZZZZZZZZZZZZZZZZZZZ
ZZZZZZZZZZZZZZZZZZZZZZZZZZZZZZZZZZZZ
ZZZZZZZZZZZZZZZZZZZZZZZZZZZZZZZZZZZZ
ZZZZZZZZZZZZZZZZZZZZZZZZZZZZZZZZZZZZ
ZZZZZZZZZZZZZZZZZZZZZZZZZZZZZZZZZZZZ

ZZZZZZZZZZZZZZZZZZZZZZZZZZZZZZZZZZZZ
ZZZZZZZAZZZZZZZZZZZZZZZZZZZZZZZZZZ
ZZZZZZZZZZZZZZZZZZZZZZZZZZZZZZZZZZZZ
ZZZZZZZZZZZZZZZZZZZZZZZZZZZZZZZZZZZZ
ZZZZZZZZZZZZZZZZZZZZZZZZZZZZZZZZZZZZ
ZZZZZZZZZZZZZZZZZZZZZZZZZZZZZZZZZZZZ
ZZZZZZZZZZZZZZZZZZZZZZZZZZZZZZZZZZZZ
ZZZZZZZZZZZZZZZZZZZZZZZZZTZZZZZZZZ
ZZZZZZZZZZZZZZZZZZZZZZZZZZZZZZZZZZZZ
ZZZZZZZZZZZZZZZZZZZZZZZZZZZZZZZZZZZZ
ZZZZZZZZZZZZZZZZZZZZZZZZZZZZZZZZZZZZ
ZZZZZZZZZZZZZZZZZZZZZZZZZZZZZZZOZZ
ZZZZZZZZZZZZZZZZZZZZZZZZZZZZZZZZZZZZ
ZZZZZZZZZZZZZZZZZZZZZZZZZZZZZZZZZZZZ
ZZZZZZZZZZZZZZZZZZZZZZZZZZZZZZZZZZZZ
ZZZZZZZZZZZZZZZZZZZZZZZZZZZZZZZZZZZZ
ZZZZZZZZZZZZZZZZZZZZZZZZZZZZZZZZZZZZ
ZZZZZZZZZZZZZZZZZZZZZZZZZZZZZZZZZZZZ
ZZZZZZZZZZZZZZZZZZZZZZZZZZZZ

You translate into well thought of.
You translate into highly regarded.

You translate into

as

it

should

be.

GLORIOUS!

Language	Ways to say glorious
Albanian	i lavdishëm
Basque	gloriosa
Bosnian	slavan
Bulgarian	славен
Catalan	gloriós
Croatian	slavan
Czech	Slavný
Danish	herlige
Dutch	glorieus
Estonian	kuulsusrikas
Finnish	mahtava
French	glorieux
Galician	glorioso
German	Herrlich
Greek	ένδοξος (éndoxos)

Language	Ways to say glorious
Hungarian	dicső
Icelandic	Glæsilega
Irish	glórmhar
Italian	glorioso
Latvian	slavens
Lithuanian	šlovingas
Macedonian	славна
Maltese	glorjużi
Norwegian	strålende
Polish	wspaniały
Portuguese	glorioso
Romanian	glorios
Russian	славный (slavnyy)
Serbian	славан (slavan)
Slovak	skvelý
Slovenian	slavno
Spanish	glorioso
Swedish	härlig
Ukrainian	славний

Language	Ways to say glorious (slavnyy)
Welsh	gogoneddus
Yiddish	כבוד

Language	Ways to say glorious
Armenian	փառավոր
Azerbaijani	şərəfli
Bengali	মহিমান্বিত
Chinese Simplified	辉煌 (huīhuáng)
Chinese Traditional	輝煌 (huīhuáng)
Georgian	დიდებული
Gujarati	ભવ્ય
Hindi	यशस्वी
Hmong	glorious
Japanese	栄光の

Language	Ways to say glorious
Kannada	ಖ್ಯಾತಿವೆತ್ತ
Kazakh	даңкты
Khmer	រុងរឿង
Korean	거룩한 (geolughan)
Lao	ອັນຮຸ່ງໂລດ
Malayalam	മഹത്തായ
Marathi	तेजस्वी
Mongolian	гайхамшигтай
Myanmar (Burmese)	ဘုန်းကြီးသော
Nepali	महिमित
Sinhala	මහිමාන්විත
Tajik	шарифи
Tamil	புகழ்பெற்ற
Telugu	అద్భుతమైన
Thai	รุ่งโรจน์

Language	Ways to say glorious
Urdu	جلالی
Uzbek	ajoyib
Vietnamese	Vinh quang

Language	Ways to say glorious
Arabic	المجيد (almajid)
Hebrew	מְפוֹאָר
Persian	با شکوه
Turkish	şanlı

Language	Ways to say glorious
Afrikaans	heerlike
Chichewa	waulemerero
Hausa	mai daraja
Igbo	dị ebube
Sesotho	e khanyang

Language	Ways to say glorious
Somali	oo ammaanta
Swahili	utukufu
Yoruba	ogo
Zulu	ekhazimulayo

Language	Ways to say glorious
Cebuano	mahimayaon
Filipino	maluwalhati
Indonesian	mulia
Javanese	kamulyane
Malagasy	be voninahitra
Malay	gemilang
Maori	kororia

Language	Ways to say glorious
Esperanto	gloraj
Haitian Creole	bèl pouvwa
Latin	gloriosum

This book is dedicated to my Parents and all that came before them, my Aunts and Uncles, to my Brother and Sister, my Nephews, my Nieces, my Cousins, my Friends and Acquaintances and every single person that I haven't met yet.

This book is also dedicated to my Sister Norma. I've also got to thank her. When I gave her some pages to read and asked her if I was on the right track, she said: "I love books like this." That was what I wanted to hear. Hugs and kisses baby sister!

You are, were,
And will always
be
glorious.

©2016 Janet Adams
All rights reserved. No part of this book shall be
reproduced, stored in a retrieval system, or
transmitted by any means, electronic, mechanical,
photocopying, recording, or otherwise without
written permission from the publisher.

www.ingramcontent.com/pod-product-compliance
Lightning Source LLC
Chambersburg PA
CBHW071435040426
42445CB00012BA/1370